Poems from Argentina

POEMS FROM ARGENTINA

David Francis

Cover photograph: Leandro Carbonell

ISBN: 978-1-950462-40-7

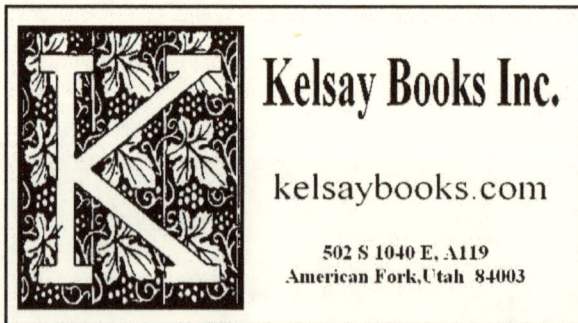

Kelsay Books Inc.

kelsaybooks.com

502 S 1040 E, A119
American Fork, Utah 84003

To the Isaac family

Acknowledgments

The author wishes to thank the editors
of the following publications:

Alba: "A Series of Locks"
Autumn Leaves: "The Song"
Carillon: "My Sadness without You"
Eskimo Pie: "The City Is Small," "The Thief," "Stream and Current," "The Dead Whale," "The Bad Comedians," "Off-Season," "The Sheep," "Fight on TV, through the Appliance Store Window," "The Ocean"
Fareham Writers: "Ushuaia"
First Literary Review-East: "A Window in front of the Mountain," "Wait, It's Loud"
Four and Twenty: "Nap"
Ink Sweat & Tears: "Tucumán Nocturne"
Lekhni: "At Evening"
Lucid Rhythms: "Apology for the Seamen"
Poetry Pacific: "The Early Morning Guard's Song," "Drops Falling after a Downpour"
River Poets Journal: "Mirror of Loneliness"
Stanzaic Stylings: "No Bluer Sky," "Lack of Lamps," "The Nervous Managers," "Reflections," "In Canning Park," "Sailboat," "San Martín de los Andes," "On the Plain," "In the Desert," "Coast Town in a Valley"
StepAway Magazine: "A River"
Swans Commentary: "The Sea Is Peaceful"
Taj Mahal Review: "The Boyish Voices"
Voices on the Wind: "In a Domesticated Suburb," "On Fire"
Whisper: "The Simple"
Ygdrasil: "Aquarium"

Most of the poems in this volume were written in 1982-83.

Contents

Tucumán

A Window in front of the Mountain

A window in front of the mountain
but from that window you cannot see
the mountain. Trees in front of fog
which is the mountain but sometimes
in front of nothing when fog
obscures the mountain. Fence posts
hold up the fence which will be
invisible every night. And the fence
posts themselves will fall if
they are not perfectly balanced and
nothing is. Clouds themselves like
towels fray and mildew, are impure
because the air is not a vacuum.
Even the cypresses will not last but
turn to sticks, a slight discolored
stain on the grass.

No Bluer Sky

No bluer sky
than that
blue dust
blue mountain
the creaking swing
the plink of hammers
from a roof
across the field
the willow curled
the parched grass
the shutters
the sound of brooms
on the white dust

A Rainy Night

The way one side (to the streetlight) of
the chimney gleams
and the tinsel of the willow
limbs boughs branches trunk gleam, too
but the wires are black
but then forms start to emerge
sharing no umbrella they hurry across
the street to one of their houses
leaving behind a house with no lights
then—the shadow of the inside of a kitchen
on a neighboring house—a face in silhouette—
in the darkness a horrible white face—
then nothing—back to bed

Tafí del Valle

Girls in bathing suits among the rocks,
trying to turn black; gold's not enough.

Forlorn and thin in the distance,
waiting for a result—there is a result.

They can turn—but only so slowly
and then must keep that position…

Their hair blows, they have it care-
fully away from their exposed faces.

They keep applying cream—but slowly and
looking at the clouds

descending on the mountains.

Pale gold is not enough. The sun
is not enough. They want

to be char. To be the darkest grass
in the darkest shadows. Damp

and oily. A strange olive,
a kind of fatigue-olive.

They want to be as dark as rags
that were once white.

But this is a lie. Guessing
is a lie.

No one knows what they want.
They spend every spare moment

in simulated deserts
and under lamps—

darkness is their enemy
and their goal.

They want white. To contrast with
and show off what they've burned.

But the most perfect among them—
the *maestras*—have no

strap lines, bathe naked
always. Just in case, in case

of the chance that sneaks into
every spent spare

fear of a second's paling,
shame of softness.

At the Edge

The child stood at the edge,
actually the curb: "Come here,
come!" A beautiful woman
walked toward her, repeating
the command, ignored. But
the child, being a child of
the city, intuitively feared
the street. She grabbed
her backward to the broad
pavement and before dragging
her away took something she
held closely, tightly: it
was two large brown
leaves big as toy boats.
With one movement
flung the leaves away.

The Early Morning Guard's Song

The steam is gone
it has served its purpose
the train is gone
either disembarking or boarding
the cows have been
cleared off the track
and led back to the
range
the sheep back
to the pasture
steam by its nature
is transient
I am resigned to that
but even the pollution
of exhaust is welcome
when it's freezing
however I am too far
from the curb
and must protect the
Platonic form of
a fort

Tucumán Nocturne

Sitting in the kitchen
with, on a tablecloth,
a notebook and a pen,
the kitchen door key hung
above the clean tile floor—
the dogs all bark at once
on the outskirts.

On the street wrought-iron
fences guard the façades
but even the nag is
tied in the nearby field
and it's not the season
for the tropical bugs
in the village.

A late autumn wind blows
down from the starless sky;
some old women walking
nod to the approaching
figure with the baby
wrapped in a bed blanket
in their hometown.

Buenos Aires

Apology for the Seamen

For seamen accustomed to such things
the world offers little surprise;
know that every person has a
passport and all the people of
one country don't look alike: there
are many types and they sometimes
cross borders. Otherwise, all
cities have the same thieves,
some of the harbors are prettier at
night. There is a logical reason
seamen are so gray and bored and
redundant and their endless card
games have the insensitive traveler's
flipping-through-postcards flatness.
There are certain calls they won't
answer and ports they wouldn't
go to if you gave them a million
dollars. They are tired of
meeting begging children on the
first land they see. Children
don't understand this.

Wait, It's Loud

Wait
it's loud
the acoustics
here
my hand
on
your breathing ribs
your eyes closed
like ribs of hair
and
your hand
reaches
for
across
over
mine

Drops Falling after a Downpour

Stick my head
                out the window
from our hotel room
                    into the alley
so dark
      with a bad smell
and feel
       the drops falling
catch one
       in my hand
one on
     my eyelid
am I
   catching
the present

29

My Sadness without You

I haven't got a breathy sadness
like a torch singer,
I've got a smooth sadness
like the choruses in Brazilian songs,
all singing the same note
without harmony.

I haven't got a strong sadness
like a soap opera actor,
I've got a weak sadness
like a man who walks down the main avenue
with the display windows,
with nothing.

I haven't got a working sadness
like a composer,
I've got a lazy sadness
like a maid who cleans up slowly,
whose husband took off,
without love.

I haven't got a mystical sadness
like a hermit-priest
but a common sadness
like a man who is disappointed,
seems to disappoint others
without knowing why.

Dark Balconies

Dark balconies
going up
that become
more and more
dark
as the night comes
and I go more and more
into myself

farther and farther
into myself
with dark balconies
to look down
and up
and see
the world
I am

leaving
but to leave something
now
to look out
but be able
to go in, always
in
looking at nothing

feeling

A River

The driving rain
pushes you further back
from the gutter
and you
begin to have a
relationship with
the people under
the same awning.

But hunger and
thirst and the
movement of the
night drive you on
to the thought that
it may continue
all night or
get stronger.

Rain slanting
that will be
at your back
like a runner
or athletic walker
leaning forward—
contemplate the other direction
farther from home.

Flowing it carries
an aerosol can
past the sewer
as it carries

my mind
and frees it—and
look there
is a current!

Lack of Lamps

In the cheap hotels
where the porter sleeps
in the stagnant air
coming through the window

in all the rooms
no matter the area
no matter the station
no matter the floor

so you cling to streetlights
you notice simple fountains
you look for the sun
you look in her eyes

someday you will ask
someday you will buy
but they will never give
they will never give

they will only give flowers
they will give the special of the day
they will give you the key
they will give you water

but there is a famine
there is a shortage
there is a lack
and you have to compensate

you have your vision
you have your hearing
you smell the food
that tastes so good

you turn the light off
you feel the darkness
you wonder about time
you sleep to wake

you listen hard sometimes
you laugh at private jokes
the darkness is without
the fire you have within

The Question

Why do you have to try so hard
just to look as if you're not completely
unhappy with me?
Don't you think I can tell
a push from a hug?
And—you don't have to jump on me
for little things—do I
do it to you?
I've always worshipped you—
do I have to name all the
habits you have that harass me?
Do you want to start something that,
one having won, we both lose?
What's wrong? Should I shut up?
You think I won't act on my threat
when I'm able to express it?
You think I came for this
from a past full of regrets?
What are you worried about?
You think I wanted this to happen—
whatever it is?
Are you sure you know what you're doing?
Are you always going to remember
something I said when I was mad?
Can't we forget about it
and live in the present?
Don't you think it's better
to be alone than to fight?
Why do you doubt—
why do you doubt me?

A Series of Locks

How far I am from my wife tonight
thinking my own thoughts
I can't hear her breathing

until she turns to me
and I think she's waking
    from her sleep
but it's me waking

The City Is Small

The city is small:
I see her on the subway
and I see her in the library.

I go out,
I think I'll return
and wait;
I try to imagine
if there are benches there.

Of course I
don't get back in time,
five minutes late;
I go looking for her
in a place near…

I'm walking, crossing
the wide avenue and the
same city is too large
though it's closing in on me.

The Consulate Library

The cleaning woman
with her moveable stairs
the one that

pushes
the chair in
with her
belly before
the man says
"young
man we're closing"

climbs them
and wipes the
shelves
with an
off-
white rag

climbing down
her
varicose veins

garters
orange

as her bucket

The Nervous Managers

A nervous man in the library
is like what we call an
"hysterical" manager of a diner
with whom to imagine to work
makes you wince, gives you
sympathy for the cooks
and ruins your meal. Or
a waiter who looks at you
funny if you order water
instead of wine or who is
in so much a hurry he
rushes off, later bringing
the wrong thing and by then
you are too hungry to exchange it.

All these owners, these ex-
military men, civilian police...

Don't they realize there are
places and moments that don't need bosses?

Aquarium

Sitting in a corner café
with a good view
on the day of the strike
except the window's closed,
a slow man comes by,
leaning, peering, taking
long looking at us,
and fills the whole
pane with his body
and his sunglasses, his cap,
his cane, with neck
turned, looking: I think
at once of the giant aquariums,
the whales and eels and those
who walk and drift at the same time.
And worse, I think
of the tentacles of a squid
in a restaurant tank,
the way he clings
to the window that displays him.

The Thief

Four apples
six plums
a hard cheese
a loaf
and a knife

on the little table
beside the bed
where they are

having their dialogue

A trouser leg
comes through the curtain
without warning

"Hey!"
pulls back

again
suddenly

"No, no…"—she—
but he
walks with the knife
to the raised window

bends out

to the right a terrified
man flat against the
façade
"What are you
doing here?"

the bread knife
clutched and ready

"Go, go away!"

The older man
cowers, confused,
maybe drunk

The younger man
stands in the middle
of the room with the knife

opens the door
and sees the man
in the hallway

"Get out of here!"

There is a door to a
balcony

but their balcony is
isolated

with a sheer drop
to the pavement

No, he didn't come
to steal

He must have come
from inside, gone
out and climbed

to their balcony

It doesn't make sense

But what if the young man
had gone out and left
his wife alone?

In disquiet and disbelief
was spent the rest
of the night

and with the cheap
dim hotel light on

the couple stared
at the knife
placed back on the table

A Quiet Find

Bottles, bottles

the hotel bar
we holed up in
waiting out
the Pope's visit
to the Capital

the screaming sirens
the crowding masses
kept away from us
by paper-thin curtains

and farther down
the national flag
draped on balconies
and on windowsills
confetti and streamers—
the Pope, the Great Arbiter...

bottles, bottles

They Sit in Shade

For a moment two old women stare
at and into each other's eyes;
one has sunglasses for the glare,
the other a summer hat but otherwise
they are unprotected from the heat
except by the café where they sit in shade
but one can't tell if they've agreed to meet
because one's already lost her cup and paid
her bill to keep water in her body
and after sat impassive as a frog
before it jumps, shaking some with palsy
yet erect as a model in a catalogue.
Not instant recognition but meditative
space between them like a memory sieve.

Hotel I Picked Earlier

Hotel I picked earlier
do you know us
old man asleep
can I pay another day
knock on the door
see you later
let him sleep
give him some peace
and us too

At Evening

As evening begins to fade
we're still sitting here
but there's a feeling it's
time to go

we begin to close
our eyes like the blind
and put fingers in fingers
praying and pulling hair
at the same time

one cannot hide feelings
from one's love
any more
than one can hide night's fall
from evening's avalanche.

In a Domesticated Suburb

When blue evening falls on
even the streetlight
that is before it
and corners start to be
mysterious obstructions
and you start to get
in the way because you
don't know the way—
earlier the grain of a
city tree caught my eye
and now again:
shops closing, people hurrying,
the awning shadows
like wave troughs,
private studies through
leaves and attracted insects,
all gold.

The Song

It's more a sad song
born of work
than the radio
and the baby
hums along

Cry
but she has a superior
patience
and transcending self-expression
asks why

You have no choice
now but to follow
and listen
to the melancholy scale
of her deep voice

Homage to Quiet Days

On quiet days the shopgirls sew
and the managers take more tea breaks,
the waitress stares more into space
and doesn't put you in your place,
the customers wander slowly as if lost,
you forget past debts or let them go,
nobody wants to be bossed,
misplaced aggressions today seem mistakes.

Stream and Current

The man's unlit cigarette
on the baby's head,
waiting for his wife
pinned by a bus,
a red light and a workers'
hole whose barricade
a narrow stream of people
has to go around,
cornered, to go right,
waits, an overlong
pause, an individual space
of belonging I flit through
like congestion at tea time.
A mother, too, hangs back
on daughter's arm, at
least it seems so in
their relation, innocent
as before in the fresh
morning when exhaust
is only the strange light.
The baby without pacifier
is lulled by movement
and possibly it is only he
who does not know the day's
movements to night.

Sad City Men

Sad city men reunite
in the same fast-food place
every night, their strange inadequate diet
a coffee just to buy a squatting space;
sometimes one sits alone and talks across
the wall to the other identical row
like people in a love seat, lost cause,
the coy separation all show
because here now it's eternally real;
sometimes move to fool the nosy boy
who picks up the trays they don't fill,
switching all night, each a decoy.

Tired of watching young lovers quarrel
and never, never accusing each other of betrayal!

Adoration of the Blind

In a faraway land in a hall waiting to be attended, the morning's appointment dragging further toward and beyond noon, I saw them lead the blind man—I can still see the awed faces and hear the attendant vacuum—it was quite a spectacle, especially as, to my knowledge, he was only physically blind.

The Diplomat's Son

Pink French walls have lost their charm
all cracked toward their high ceilings
and if Dad loses the farm
it won't hurt my feelings

Like a famous athlete
who's been all round the world
it's always the same old street
despite the flag unfurled

Marie just died, the one we had
the new one's Jacqueline
occasionally it makes me sad
to think of her again

I'm thinking of giving up collecting
though my collection's worth a lot
I think I've collected everything
from African ore to carat

My walls are filled with posters
my mirror with photographs
my dresser's got souvenir coasters
I break them just for laughs

These high balconies could do me harm
and though I've got money I steal things
but if Dad loses the farm
it won't hurt my feelings

Waking

Back of a woman playing Ping-Pong
but the sound of workers.

A man with a tie
standing in a window.
Now a girl waving.

The transparent curtain blowing
wildly in the room.
A man sitting with hands behind his head.

The elbow of a pipe.

The Boyish Voices

I can see through the shutters
reflections that shouldn't be there
and I can hear the wind
blow the beautiful city tree leaves down;
I can see a sidewalk weed sprout
and a man with baggy pants—all wet—
watching the boyish voices.

It's dark in the cheap hotel room
without reading lamps
and it's late in the evening;
all day the trucks that drown out conversation
at night lull to sleep,
a sleep too deep to hear the maid's knock
on the Day of Rest.

Now the sound of the shared pat of the ball
again and the different sound it makes
as it bounces on the wet pavement
and then they go over a stoop.
The rain stops.
I open the window to let in air
and find the sill is higher than I thought.

Reflections

Never has she looked lovelier
nor I felt lonelier
we came to the café to discuss
and now I can't even begin
to bring up the truth
we can only bear
to look at each other's reflection

Ode to a Man in an Alley

A man
walks through
a long corridor
through latticework
and open arches
to join
others
on the
street
lost

I go
back
by
a car
opening
door
to
see
him
black
protected
from
sunlight

a
winding
stairway
with
chain
shadows
a
rotting
smell

badly
upholstered
chairs
sky
shooting
through
a
skylight

through
hoops
toward
a
ticket
window
the
woman
cleaning
the
man
doesn't
wait
for
the
question

without
sleep
the
voice
says
No

his narrow world
his territory
the echoes his
he comes with
his projection
but always
receding

I go back
but
without sleep
the answer
is
No

for the moment
protected
from
the
sunlight
of
poverty
in
the
restful
afternoon
in
the
alley

but
coming
to
join

but
for the moment
always
receding

the
longer
moment
says
nothing
asleep

I go back
one
eye
closed
sees
a
different
picture

the
other
eye
won't
go

he
is
thrown
back
into

the
back
of
the
corridor
the
latticework
shatters
to
leaves
in
the
underground
wind
he
floats
forward

at
home

The Dead Whale

There is a dead whale on the sidewalk.
Strange no one has noticed.
There it sprawls, black on the
white pavement.
If it were newly-laid cement
it would leave quite a print.
Well, the port breeze is so strong
you can't catch the scent.
The other day there was a swarm of
dragonflies—people are getting
used to plagues of creatures.
The difference is this is
one big individual.
His eyes are as open as the dead.
Why is it I have a feeling he was blind?
How do I know? Just an intuition.
It doesn't matter.
The only hope of moving him
is if someone comes along
and pries open his mouth to
see the strange things he's swallowed.
There's no telling what kind
of person that will be.
Someone very determined
who's not afraid of death.
Maybe a medical student.
Maybe a folklorist.
A strange thing to see,
the last day of the week;
a strange way to begin a weekend!
What a strange sight!
What a curious person!

The Eye

Attracted by the spiked leaf
growing out of the ground
the dragonfly will come back
several times, still bi-plane
the cat knows this
as he sidles up
to the plant through grass
his head turned by a distraction
closer tail wagging
because he knows this
dragonfly straight up like a helicopter
watches disinterestedly
body tense—concentrated—
coiled for the leap—
one chance
because his enemy's bored—
now!—misses—
blown back by gravity
like another leaf

In Canning Park

They have the names of the plants—
all exotic Latin names and origins—
but where are the plants?
Have the seeds blown away in this strong wind
or are they out of season?

Cats curl up in the holes
where mongrel full-grown trees protect them,
and roll over slowly to scratch their backs
but when the sun moves the sun- and tree-round shade
they go to sunbathe.

Sometimes the young go to the old
for something they can't get on the street;
with all of its new coffee shops and chain stores
it still can't offer this womblike timelessness
when you're in the mood.

Nap

Old man nodding
assenting to
something I fear

The Simple

The simple are not the simple
and the complicated are a sickening cycle
and you can't understand anything because of the spinning

Fate is not fate
and chance is like luck's wheel
and necessity makes you throw the dice when you don't know the
prize

The past is not past
and the future is a shopping list
and the present haunts you with everyone and everything it wants
to

The pure is not pure
and the mixture won't merge into a flavor
so you add something old trying again to make gold

Love is not love
and hate says you're a living failure
but both can die because emotional success is anybody's guess

The simple are not the simple
and the complicated are a sickening cycle
when they say they're simple don't believe till you see an example

Mar del Plata

On Fire

Just as in the woods
the charred remains of a
campfire mean someone
has been there,
so, too, a few clothes
on the beach—
shoes, socks and towel
in the middle of all that sand,
a clearing surrounded by
skyscrapers, hotels and jetties.
And just as from the woods
one approaches the char,
curious and sympathetic
to see foreign life there,
a woman comes from the tide,
unhindered by stumps and
thorns but heavy in the
sand, and stands and waits
for the child and man—
still at the edge of the
clearing that is in this
case the horizon—
she has come with who
claim and carry their warmth,
leaving no particular burnt site,
no charred remains of life.

Surface of the Living

Wire, string and rock on the beach
and cork—and tops—
not all of it buried yet
and rope of course—
what slipped through hands

and here I've found
a noose on a pole
or just a knot
and a stick as one
would find on the ground

all under webs

Sailboat

Man on a sailboat
stretched out like a starfish
controlling the sail
but it starts to fall
and he loses it
flat on the waves
and then a shadow
falls over the beach
with his back bowed
he pulls the ropes
him against the sea
him against the wind
and another shadow falls
and he raises it
no one has noticed
but out of shame
the sun went behind the clouds

now in the distance
closer to the horizon
you see a man
play tug of war
with a sail
and then you see him sail

The Beach Photographer

Even though he's a pest
I felt sorry for him
everyone was depressed
the day sunk in boredom

walking in bare feet
with his camera strap
walking in the heat
instead of a nap

climbing the stone steps
without any cash
and looking so inept
carrying his flash

but then he leaned against
the entrance to the pier
in his wrinkled pants
and stared straight over here

the sun began to thrive
he held his postcard like a visor
it made him more alive
to look into that glare

The Bad Comedians

The bad comedians
face the front,
shouting,
forgetting their lines
for the old
in the audience
with crow's feet
and bad teeth
and styled hair,
they have lived
the same years;
the straight man
started as a
vaudeville straight man
and now has
his own show;
as a filler
he uses his
old vaudeville friends
who do the
same old routines
they did when
show business started;
the band plays
during the break
after which the
bad comedians introduce
and interview the
new singers and
stylists and authorities:
too much description,

isn't it—just
to convey the
truth of the
bad comedians' lives?

Off-Season

The only thing that can make her laugh
is the comics
not my faces
not my vaudeville routines
not my puns
not my sense of humor
so I bought her some comics
as long as they keep putting them out
we'll survive

Mirror of Loneliness

The loneliest rooms facing the sea
the opposite of what people say
the sea is a mirror of loneliness
once a week the old
go out for coffee
always the same room
always the curtains open
the bricks discolored
and the railings black
and the sea that was green this morning
too ripe with age
and I look up and see
the same man in the day
that I saw at night
and dirty gulls fly in the dirty clouds
and an old man walks his dog
runs him across the street
then takes off the leash
and sets him free
     on the beach
and the man picks up the bread
for the birds and throws it
and the little dog ignores him
     for a sand castle

The Sea Is Peaceful

Always armies and navies
young men marching
drafted and career
going into sea towns
on the weekend
no one looks so
lonely; child
generals imagining
enemies on the horizon
pirates of other bureaucracies
oh we say the sea
is violent
but it's just an expression
the sea is peaceful
but always, always
old waves rolling
young men marching,
young men.

Honeymoon Hitchhike

Through a Field in a City

Through someone's sleepy neighborhood
of continuous cement houses
whose shadows are themselves
the shadows pause forever
and the early afternoon sun
bakes black dirt hills dry
and crinkles littered cans,
a cactus here and there
among cracked and cracking mounds
and the street's traffic sounds.

San Martín de los Andes

The angle of the lake
reflecting blue sky and white clouds
smack up against the bluff—
sharp as the cold.

The khaki-colored buildings
hawking the indigenous,
honeycombed with tourists.

Icy air and the sun
on the pebble-bottomed water
lapping, lapping
at eventide.

My young bride climbs in beneath the horsehair!

The Sheep

He says "Bah" loudly like
a grouchy man who has
the face of an idiot.
His eyes are far apart
and his snout is long.
He is big and drags
a chain through a pasture.
He goes into the ditch.
We are leaving the town.
He sticks his tongue out.

Provincial Bank

The man removes his hat
upon entering the bank
as if in a church
there's Someone to thank.

Her address the woman
can't remember;
as a courtesy
they fingerprint her.

The old and the poor
wait in the back.
At the tellers the grown-up
bad schoolboys attack.

On the Plain

The wind has drowned out the footsteps
behind me
and the telephone lines
go my way
like trees beside a road—
I am looking for
the ones that cross.
I see tall buildings in the distance:
there's nothing to obscure them.
I realize the past is not
what I want; but I'm lonely.
I want to stop.
I want to go back.
I'm tempted to.

But I have to catch up,
carrying a heavy load.

In the Desert

little pine struggling
with its baby arms
to tie itself to
the hitching post
and not be blown
so hard by the
wind

a tall pole
with a feeder
tilts

in the distance
gray mountains

it didn't take
root
but was planted,
the little pine

O wind that causes
hallucinations

at least
give it the dignity
of a horse!

Fight on TV, through the Appliance Store Window

In a corner
the boxer so beaten
he doesn't know he's sitting

they pour water on him
he's rained on
he's blind

poor dumb brute
lover of
fighting

that's the part I don't like
when there's no balance
when it's lopsided

in a corner
on a stool
the legs sawn through

as though a drinking contest
with an audience
urging him on

as though a bachelor party
with his friends
he hasn't seen for years

like the lover
who, too, must continue
because it's all he's got

A Wall in Río Gallegos

Woman in black walking along the white wall,
holding her purse tightly as though in a stall,
ignoring the signs advertising the city
as though they were so much graffiti,
huddling in the chill of the South
with an inward face and unpuckered mouth;
she might as well be a beached whale on sand,
something in an environment it doesn't understand;
I had seen her before proudly enter the café
as the men froze their dice and glowered her way:
what made her move to this cold town
like a black rose by a sudden snow weighed down?

The Ocean

We stood on the long hopeless road
out of the horrible industrial small town
in between the place where they check the trucks
and millions of hills going south.
We had crossed the country in one day
and had taken all day to walk out of a city;
now here we were on a Sunday
with no traffic during no vacation season.
When one sits long one has to entertain
oneself with humor, reminiscences and songs
and try to make the hours seem one hour
and try to forget about the fading sun.
So when nothing came we hopped across the field
beyond which was the ocean without a beach
where junk and weeds made the eroding edge
and far-off derricks pumped away the sludge.
Listening for wheels we began to hum
and then again silent with the despair of patience
and started to run when we saw the dust flying
to beg in the middle of nowhere to be wafted.

Coast Town in a Valley

Rays come down
geese honk above the flat lake
    reflecting the mountains
lichens slant
    toward town

A northern house with a
    sharp, sturdy roof
starts the town
    only one skyscraper
    spoils the horizon
on either side
    coast and cove
not blurred
    but made blue

fog in the valley

on the hill
    a leveled fence
and unknown burrows
    footholds

stepping between the wires
    and overlooking

sliding falling running
    down mud
to roadside flowers

the wind blowing
  the clouds blackening
    but passing

and then out of the sea
　　like oil
a few colors shoot

straight up
over or through
rays

and end
　　in brown inland

only the ends

somehow in a moment
　　the sky clears
　　and you see
　　the rainbow

Ushuaia

I. In the South near the Border

A sheared mess on the grass.
The dirty birds—the kind no one eats
or keeps for pets
or has in his barnyard—
cross the green and white wild grasses.
The sky is filled to the brim
with white entangled clouds.
The road is black with recent mud.
Otherwise, stone shoulders.
Horses with dull brands.

II. On the Ferry

Clouds move like a dust storm behind the station behind us
the lighthouse blinks and the antennas are fine
what seemed to be stopped
and even going backward from the shore is fast
my cold breath goes out
the porthole and adds nothing
as light on the coast blinks back

III. No Reflections

Though the water is not frozen
it is still not a mirror
because the bank saves the snow
and only the streetlights are reflected
widened like a foundation

the shadow of the stovepipe
on the snow is like a toadstool
but neither the frozen wires
nor the frozen antenna
that balances like a cat

have shadows or reflections
and the reason is
buried things have no reflection
and the snow buries
even the clouds

sometimes even the stars

IV. Outside by the Ocean

A twisted tree
on the side of a hill
and behind a yellow falling torrent
and bushes with orange thorns
stranded on streaked snow
sea gulls congregate on an isthmus
and cows listen
strange buds start reddening
one ahead of the others
in the distance
ready

About the Author

Born in Houston, David Francis has lived in London, Buenos Aires, and New York. He has produced six music albums, one of poetry, and *Always/Far,* a chapbook of lyrics and drawings. In 2008 the publication of his essay "Utterance and Hum: The Difference between Poem and Song" led to a lecture tour of the UK. In addition, he has written and directed the films *Village Folksinger* (2013) and *Memory Journey* (2018). His poems and short stories have appeared in a number of journals and anthologies.

www.davidfrancismusic.com

Kelsay Books